Generations

My Family Treasure
Preserving the Story, History and Facts
of My Family

RICHARD A. GAINES

ISBN: 978-0-578-02088-4

Contents

Dedication

I would like to dedicate this book to Family, Friends and Future Generations.

Introduction

Let this book become a lasting and beautiful treasure for your children, grandchildren and generations far into the future. Your personal recollections are priceless and will carry so much more meaning for your family more so than any book you may have on your bookshelves. Take your time to think, feel and believe in the treasure that is Your Family.

Remember the only constant in life is change. You will be recording changes from childhood to adulthood, from being single to being married, from work to retirement and much more. You will document the passage from one phase of life to another, and it will always include a period of transition. We need to hear about our families -- and our children need to hear from us. From our everyday rituals to stories of daunting success and impressive achievements, wisdom comes from understanding and revealing our family's dreams and beliefs. As we look back at how our ancestors faced the challenges and changes in their lives, it gives us inspiration to look forward to our future and our children's future.

As you write your thoughts and memories in your own handwriting, you leave an imprint of yourself in this special book. Similar to a scrapbook, we have intentionally left blank areas on pages for you to attach clippings, photos and drawings. We have also included a Family Portrait as an appendix. Have fun and enjoy recording the people, stories and times of your family's lives!

1. Great-Great Grandparents

What are the full names of your great great-grandparents? What have you learned about them?What was their native country and where did they live as children? What do you know about their day-to-day lives?Do you know what work or employment they did to support their families?

Maternal Side

_____

_____

_____

_____

_____

_____

_____

Paternal Side

_____

_____

_____

_____

_____

_____

_____

2. Great Grandparents

What were the full names of your great grandparents? What have you learned about your great grandparents? Where were they born and live as children? What do you know about their day-to-day lives? What type of work did they do to support their families?

Maternal Side

_____

_____

_____

_____

_____

_____

_____

Paternal Side

_____

_____

_____

_____

_____

_____

_____

Write down one or two of the stories they told you or your parents about what is was like being a child and growing up in the 1800s or early 1900s.

_____

_____

_____

_____

_____

_____

_____

3. Grandparents

What were the full names of your grandparents? What do you know about your grandparents' background and lives? Where were they born and live as children? What do you know about their day-to-day lives? What work did they do to support their families?

Maternal Side

_____

_____

_____

_____

_____

_____

Paternal Side

_____

_____

_____

_____

_____

_____

Did you ever talk with your grandparents about their lives or your parents' lives? If so, what personal information did they share with you?

_____

_____

_____

_____

_____

_____

_____

Do you remember anything about your grandparents' brothers and sisters? Did you have a favorite great aunt or great uncle?If you did, why were they special?

_____

_____

_____

_____

_____

_____

_____

Have your grandparents told you how much different today's world is from when they were growing up? Write down a few of the ways times have changed.

_____

_____

_____

_____

_____

_____

_____

4. Parents

What are the full names of your mother and father? Where were your parents born and raised? What were the neighborhoods like in which they grew up? How do they describe their homes and schools?

_____

_____

_____

_____

_____

_____

_____

What do your parents say about how the world has changed from what it was like when they were growing up as kids?

_____

_____

_____

_____

_____

_____

_____

What do you know about your mother's early years? Who brought her up and what have you learned about how she was raised? Was she brought up in a family environment with financial stress or one of wealth?

_____

_____

_____

_____

_____

_____

_____

How did your mother spend her day? Did she stay at home? Did she need to go to work to help your family make ends meet? Or, did she go to work just because she wanted to have her own career?

_____

_____

_____

_____

_____

_____

_____

What do you know about your father's early years? Who brought him up and what have you learned about how he was raised? Was he brought up in a family environment with financial stress or one of wealth?

_____

_____

_____

_____

_____

_____

_____

How did your father spend his day? Did he work or stay at home?

_____

_____

_____

_____

_____

_____

_____

Take a moment to go back to your childhood and describe your mother and father as you recall seeing them together?

_____

_____

_____

_____

_____

_____

_____

Where did your mother and/or father go to work? What were their career(s) or job(s)?

_____

_____

_____

_____

_____

_____

_____

Did they change jobs or careers during your childhood? If so, did you have to move because of this job change?

_____

_____

_____

_____

_____

_____

_____

5. Siblings

What are your brothers and sisters full names? How old were you when each was born? Do you recall how you felt at the time? Do you think your birth order gives any clues about your individual personalities?

_____

_____

_____

_____

_____

_____

_____

Talk about one special memory about each of your brothers and sisters.

_____

_____

_____

_____

_____

_____

6. Aunt and Uncles

What are your aunts and uncles names? What role did they play in your life? Did you get together on holidays or for special family gatherings? Do you remain in touch with them?

_____

_____

_____

_____

_____

_____

_____

7. Cousins

What are your cousins' names? What role did they play in your life? Did you get together on holidays or for special family gatherings? Do you remain in touch with them?

_____

_____

_____

_____

_____

_____

_____

8. Nieces / Nephews

What are the full names of your nieces and nephews? Do you consider yourself to be close with any of them? Are there any fond memories of time spent with them?

_____

_____

_____

_____

_____

_____

9. Stepfamilies

What is your stepmother's full name and birthplace?

_____

_____

_____

_____

_____

_____

How did you meet your new stepmother?

_____

_____

_____

_____

_____

_____

_____

What are her unique character and personality traits?

_____

_____

_____

_____

_____

_____

What is your stepfather's name and birthplace?

_____

_____

_____

_____

_____

_____

How did you meet your new stepfather?

_____

_____

_____

_____

_____

_____

_____

What are his unique character and personality traits?

_____

_____

_____

_____

_____

_____

What characteristics do you admire the most about your stepmom and/or stepdad? Did he/she bring any new traditions into your family?

_____

_____

_____

_____

_____

_____

Stepsiblings - do you have any stepsisters and/or stepbrothers? What are their names and ages?

_____
_____
_____
_____
_____
_____
_____

What traits do your stepsiblings have in common with you? What characteristics make them different from you?

_____
_____
_____
_____
_____
_____
_____

When you were growing up, did your stepsiblings live with you? Have you blended your stepsiblings into your existing one?

_____
_____
_____
_____
_____
_____
_____

Half-Siblings -- Do you have half-sisters or half-brothers? What are their names and ages? How did you get along with them?

_____

_____

_____

_____

_____

_____

_____

Do you have any special memories of them?

_____

_____

_____

_____

_____

_____

10. Adopted Families

What is your biological mother's name, birthplace and siblings?

_____

_____

_____

_____

_____

_____

Do you know any specific family background or information about her life and career?

_____

_____

_____

_____

_____

_____

What is your biological father's name, birthplace and siblings?

_____

_____

_____

_____

_____

_____

Do you know any specific family background or information about his life and career?

_____

_____

_____

_____

_____

_____

_____

11. Country of Origin

Do you know when your first family members came to America? Where did they come from? Where did your ancestors first land? Where did they settle? Where did they move? Do any family members still live abroad?

_____
_____
_____
_____
_____
_____
_____

Are there stories of a harrowing event of travel from the old country to America?

_____
_____
_____
_____
_____
_____

What generation of American are you?

_____
_____
_____
_____
_____
_____

What nationalities are you? What physical traits do you exhibit that can be attributed to a certain country or ancestry?

_____

_____

_____

_____

_____

_____

_____

12. Your Family Name

Your family name links you to your ancestors. Exploring the origins of your family name can shed light on the people who have come before you. What do you know about your family name? What is its origin? Was it taken from the bible . . . a name of a town . . . an occupation?

_____

_____

_____

_____

_____

_____

_____

Are there any ancestors remembered for being famous? What facts about their lives might be considered notable? Did any of them play a role in history? Were there any actors . . . writers . . . athletes . . . political figures?

_____

_____

_____

_____

_____

_____

_____

Can you track your family name to a country of origin?

_____

_____

_____

_____

_____

_____

_____

Do you have a family coat of arms? Does your name mean something in a foreign language?

_____

_____

_____

_____

_____

_____

Modifying a family name was common when immigrants arrived in the United States. Do you know if your family's original name was changed?

_____

_____

_____

_____

_____

_____

_____

If it was changed, do any of your current relatives use the original family name? Have any of your family members used the original name as a first or middle name for their children?

_____

_____

_____

_____

_____

_____

_____

What are your mother's, grandmother's and great grandmother's maiden names?

_____

_____

_____

_____

_____

_____

_____

What are your father's, grandfather's and great grandfather's last names?

_____

_____

_____

_____

_____

_____

_____

Do you know if you were named after a relative, famous person or someone else? Was there any significance to your name and its meaning?

_____
_____
_____
_____
_____
_____
_____

Does your family have a naming tradition?

_____
_____
_____
_____
_____
_____

If you were named for a family member, what traits do family members tell you that you have in common with your namesake?

_____
_____
_____
_____
_____
_____

Were any of your siblings named for family members and, if so, do they share any characteristics with the relative they were named for?

_____

_____

_____

_____

_____

_____

_____

Do you know if you have any family members have brought fame to your family name? If so, who and what did they do to become famous?

_____

_____

_____

_____

_____

_____

_____

What is your spouse or partner's full name? Did their family come from a particular part of the world?

_____

_____

_____

_____

_____

_____

Does your spouse or partner's name have any special meaning?

_____

_____

_____

_____

_____

_____

Are there names in your spouse's family that have particular significance?

_____

_____

_____

_____

_____

How did you determine your children's names? What do they mean? Do their names play into your family history?

_____

_____

_____

_____

_____

_____

What nicknames did you give your children, if any?

_____

_____

_____

_____

_____

_____

_____

How were your grandchildren's names chosen?

_____

_____

_____

_____

_____

_____

_____

13. Family Wisdom and Stories

Did your grandparents and parents share their philosophy of life with you? If so, what was it?

_____

_____

_____

_____

_____

_____

_____

Of all the things your parents/grandparents shared with you, which do you feel was the most important and valuable?

_____

_____

_____

_____

_____

_____

What lesson did they feel passionate about passing along? What lessons are you making sure you pass on to your children/grandchildren?

_____

_____

_____

_____

_____

_____

Write about a special memory of your grandparents or an older individual you admired and loved. Is there an aunt, uncle, cousin or close family friend who ignites a special childhood memory?

_____

_____

_____

_____

_____

_____

_____

Of their accomplishments -- which ones do you think your great grandparents and grandparents would say they were most proud?

_____

_____

_____

_____

_____

_____

_____

What role have those achievements played in inspiring your life goals?

_____

_____

_____

_____

_____

_____

_____

What would each of your parents say were their greatest achievements?

_____

_____

_____

_____

_____

_____

_____

What role have their accomplishments served in creating your life goals?

_____

_____

_____

_____

_____

_____

What time in their lives would your mother and father say was their most challenging? Why was it difficult for them?

_____

_____

_____

_____

_____

_____

Do you know if they ever suffered a great loss? If so, how did they recover from the sadness? How did it impact you?

_____

_____

_____

_____

_____

_____

_____

Think of a time when you were younger when something sad or disappointing happened. Did your grandparents and/or parents share their hard-earned wisdom to help you cope with the difficult situation?

_____

_____

_____

_____

_____

_____

_____

14. Wars and Military Service

What wars have been fought during your ancestors' lifetime? Did your great grandparents, grandparents and/or parents serve in the military? If so, in what service, when and where did they serve? What were their duties?

_____

_____

_____

_____

_____

_____

_____

15. Special Interests, Hobbies, Sports and Music

What were your parents' and grandparents' favorite hobbies? Do you share any of these hobbies?

_____

_____

_____

_____

_____

_____

_____

Have members of your family followed one another in the same profession or a particular pursuit?

_____

_____

_____

_____

_____

_____

_____

Did your grandparents or parents excel at a certain sport? If so, which one?

_____

_____

_____

_____

_____

_____

_____

Do you or anyone in your immediate or extended family play a musical instrument? Is it a tradition to have them entertain at family gatherings?

_____

_____

_____

_____

_____

_____

_____

Are there any special talents that seem to run in your family? Did your grandparents and parents exhibit a passion for art, music or ability to write? Has anyone in the family ever been recognized for these talents?

_____

_____

_____

_____

_____

_____

_____

16. Passion and Happiness

Do you have a particular passion that you share with your family members? What is it? How and who do you believe helped inspire and mentor you in passion?

_____

_____

_____

_____

_____

_____

_____

Did any of your relatives choose happiness and passion over security to follow their dreams? If so, what did they do? How has that choice influenced your life?

_____

_____

_____

_____

_____

_____

_____

Did you have favorite games or hobbies that you shared with your family members as a child? Did your family members laugh a lot?

---

17. Discoveries and Inventions

In addition to the computer, what would you consider to be the most important inventions made during your ancestors' lifetimes?

_____

_____

_____

_____

_____

_____

_____

18. Family Tree Famous Relatives

Were any of your family members well-known or local/national celebrities?

_____

_____

_____

_____

_____

_____

_____

What brought them recognition and success?

_____

_____

_____

_____

_____

_____

_____

Did anyone in your family exhibit extraordinary talents or abilities? Did they win awards? Were they featured on television, radio or in the media?

_____

_____

_____

_____

_____

_____

_____

19. Occupations and Careers

What professions run in your family? Do you see a trend from your grandparents to your parents? Are there any interesting professions like chefs, artists, weavers, movie producers, stage set designers . . . ?

_____

_____

_____

_____

_____

_____

_____

What is your career and profession? When and how did you choose it?

_____

_____

_____

_____

_____

_____

_____

20. Distinguishing Family Traits, Characteristics and Beliefs

What characteristics . . . intellectual, physical, emotional or spiritual have your children inherited from you or other family members?

_____

_____

_____

_____

_____

_____

_____

On your mother's side of the family, what personality traits and/or beliefs do your parents say your great-grandparents and grandparents handed down to your family?

_____

_____

_____

_____

_____

_____

_____

On your father's side of the family, what traits, characteristics and/or beliefs serve as the legacy your great-grandparents and grandparents handed down to your family?

_____

_____

_____

_____

_____

_____

_____

On your mother's side of the family, share one of the traits you admired most about your grandmother. Name a trait that impressed you the most about your grandfather.

_____

_____

_____

_____

_____

_____

_____

On your father's side of the family, name one of the traits you admired most about your grandmother. Write about the personality trait that impressed you the most about your grandfather.

_____

_____

_____

_____

_____

_____

_____

Are there any of these distinguishing characteristics that you believe you share with your ancestors? Do people remark that you share the gift of gab, sense of humor or other personality trait with any of your relatives?

_____

_____

_____

_____

_____

_____

_____

How similar are the physical resemblances in your family? Are there certain features, such as color of eyes, shape of head, facial moles, hair, height etc. that many family members seem to share?

_____

_____

_____

_____

_____

_____

Are there certain verbal expressions many family members use?

_____

_____

_____

_____

_____

_____

What was the funniest or silliest thing you ever saw one of your older relatives do? Why was it so funny?

_____

_____

_____

_____

_____

_____

_____

What admirable qualities do you find in close family members?

_____

_____

_____

_____

_____

_____

_____

List three words that describe the personalities of each your family members. Include both of your grandparents, your parents, yourself, your aunts and uncles, your siblings, your children and your grandchildren. What are the similarities and differences?

_____

_____

_____

_____

_____

_____

_____

What connections do you see exist between the generations?

_____

_____

_____

_____

_____

_____

_____

21. Friends and Neighbors

Can you remember an especially interesting family friend(s)? A person or couple who frequently visited your home? What made the person(s) or occasions memorable for you?

_____

_____

_____

_____

_____

_____

_____

Who were your family's favorite neighbors? As a child growing up who were your favorite neighbors?

_____

_____

_____

_____

_____

_____

_____

Who were your mother and father's everyday friends? What do you remember that was so special about them? Were they baseball buddies, regular card players, sports enthusiasts, car pooling, companions etc.?

_____

_____

_____

_____

_____

_____

Do you find you have similar friends in your life today?

_____

_____

_____

_____

_____

Who was your best childhood friend? Give when and where information.

_____

_____

_____

_____

_____

_____

What did you most enjoy doing with this person?

_____

_____

_____

_____

_____

_____

_____

22. Special Times and Events

What is your earliest memory of your maternal and paternal grandparents? What do you know about them from the stories you heard from your parents?

_____

_____

_____

_____

_____

_____

Do you remember your family discussing world politics and events that influenced your great grandparents' or grandparents' lives?

_____

_____

_____

_____

_____

_____

Do you know if your ancestors went through any tough times or struggles? How did what they went through encourage, inspire or help you?

_____

_____

_____

_____

_____

_____

_____

Did your family go through any transitions or changes when you were a child? It might have been a divorce, loss of job and/or death of a family member? How did the situation affect you at the time? What life lessons did it teach you?

_____

_____

_____

_____

_____

_____

_____

What family life events do you feel have had a major impact or influence on your life?

_____

_____

_____

_____

_____

_____

_____

Because of your family experiences, what accomplishments do you think you can attribute to your growth in this area?

_____

_____

_____

_____

_____

_____

_____

23. Family Secrets

What don't tell your mother secrets have your grandparents or aunts and uncles shared with you?

_____

_____

_____

_____

_____

_____

_____

Are there any family skeletons in the closet stories?

_____

_____

_____

_____

_____

_____

Every family has black sheep. Who are considered the black sheep in your family? Do you talk to them or about them?

_____

_____

_____

_____

_____

_____

Have your aunt and uncles shared any good stories about your mother's and father's childhoods? How they were in school? What they did to get in trouble with their parents?

_____

_____

_____

_____

_____

_____

_____

Do you have any secret stories about your own childhood?

_____

_____

_____

_____

_____

_____

24. Languages

Did your great grandparents or grandparents speak a language other than English? Did they often talk about life in the old country? If so, what did like about it, and why did they not go back?

_____

_____

_____

_____

_____

_____

_____

Did your family speak more than one language in the home when you were growing up? Was it confusing to you, or did you find it a positive influence?

_____

_____

_____

_____

_____

_____

_____

25. Fashion and Fads

In your grandparents' day what fads were popular? From hairstyles to clothes to entertainment . . . what about in your parents' day?

_____

_____

_____

_____

_____

_____

_____

Share what hairstyles, fashion, games, entertainment, music, etc., were popular when you were young? Do your children copy any of them today?

_____

_____

_____

_____

_____

_____

_____

Have your grandparents discussed what changes they have seen over their lifetime? What did they especially like and dislike?

_____

_____

_____

_____

_____

_____

_____

26. Religion and Spiritual Beliefs

Did your ancestors practice any particular religion? Do you practice it today? Explain why or why not.

_____

_____

_____

_____

_____

_____

_____

What about your spouse's family? What is their religious heritage?

_____

_____

_____

_____

_____

_____

_____

How did your grandparents pass down their spiritual heritage to your parents and to you?

_____

_____

_____

_____

_____

_____

_____

What piece of wisdom that came from the heart did they share with you?

_____

_____

_____

_____

_____

_____

_____

Many families include mixed marriages -- people of different religions, ethnic, racial or sexual orientations marry. Are there mixed marriages in your family?

_____

_____

_____

_____

_____

_____

_____

Has your immediate family accepted or rejected the mixed marriage couples and their relationships?

_____

_____

_____

_____

_____

_____

_____

Were any of your ancestors people of God i.e. rabbis, priests, ministers, clerics or missionaries? Of what denomination and where did they serve?

_____

_____

_____

_____

_____

_____

_____

As a young adult did you take part in any religious groups, scout troops or sports teams where the leaders played a key role in influencing your life?

_____

_____

_____

_____

_____

_____

If so, who were these role models? Explain how they inspired you.

_____

_____

_____

_____

_____

_____

Do you have any spiritually-related memories you'd like to share? Has anyone in your life mentioned having a NDE or Near Death Experience?

_____

_____

_____

_____

_____

_____

_____

27. Education

Did your parents and other older relatives attend the same school?

_____

_____

_____

_____

_____

_____

_____

What level of education did your grandparents and parents have? Which of them went on to achieve advanced degrees?

_____

_____

_____

_____

_____

_____

_____

Did your family produce any renowned scholars or scientists?

_____

_____

_____

_____

_____

_____

Did your ancestors pass their love of knowledge down to you?

_____

_____

_____

_____

_____

_____

_____

How far did you have to travel to school? How did you get there?

_____

_____

_____

_____

_____

_____

_____

Did your brothers and sisters attend the same school?

_____

_____

_____

_____

_____

_____

_____

What is your most vivid and compelling school memory?

_____

_____

_____

_____

_____

_____

_____

Who was your favorite teacher and what subject did the person teach? How did he or she encourage you and draw out your best talents?

_____

_____

_____

_____

_____

_____

_____

What after-school club activities and sports did you participate in?Did you ever win any awards for your studies, school or sports activities?

_____

_____

_____

_____

_____

_____

_____

How were your grades? Did you like school or find it hard? How do your children like school?

_____

_____

_____

_____

_____

_____

_____

What level of school did you complete? Give the who, what, where and when about your education.

_____

_____

_____

_____

_____

_____

_____

28. Family Stories and Memories

Stories shape and define our history -- who we are. Every family has a story. One passed down from parent to child for generations. In these tales ancestors sometime accomplish amazing feats, such as being the first man to climb Mt. Everest; or your grand uncle invented the first snowmobile; or your cousin ran away to Paris to paint world famous artwork. What is your family special story?

_____

_____

_____

_____

_____

_____

_____

Of all your family stories who is the character you most identify with and why? What was your favorite part of the story? Was there a moral to the story? If so, what was it?

_____

_____

_____

_____

_____

_____

_____

How much of this story do you think is true? How much is fiction? If this story is based on actual facts, what were the facts?

_____

_____

_____

_____

_____

_____

_____

Is there a wonderful love story that's been passed down? How your grandparents met or your great aunt never married after her fiancé died during World War II?

_____

_____

_____

_____

_____

_____

Are there any particular sayings you remember your grandparents or relatives repeating? What are the phrases, like Abe is a smart cookie? When did they pop up in conversations?

_____

_____

_____

_____

_____

_____

Did you hear tales about distant ancestors who were famous or infamous? What were they?

_____

_____

_____

_____

_____

_____

_____

Every family seems to boast about an ancestor with an interesting or spotted past. Who was the wild and crazy ancestor in your family? What did this person do to warrant his/her reputation?

_____

_____

_____

_____

_____

_____

_____

What are some of the other outlandish tales you have heard about family members? Is there a myth surrounding anyone in particular? A great uncle who was a prince or second cousin who skated as Mickey Mouse in Disney On Ice?

_____

_____

_____

_____

_____

_____

_____

What stories do your parents share about the day of your birth?

_____

_____

_____

_____

_____

_____

_____

What are some of their favorite memories of your childhood?

_____

_____

_____

_____

_____

_____

List a few of your favorite books -- ones read to you by grand-parents or parents?

_____

_____

_____

_____

_____

_____

What stories or books do you pass on to your children, nieces and nephews today?

_____

_____

_____

_____

_____

_____

Write about a special outing you took with one or both of your parents?

_____

_____

_____

_____

_____

_____

Paint a brief picture of what has been the happiest time of your life?

_____

_____

_____

_____

_____

_____

Describe in detail what is your happiest family memory?

_____

_____

_____

_____

_____

_____

_____

Recall a particularly happy-go-lucky time during your teenage years. Describe why and how you felt. As you think about it, how does looking back make you feel today?

_____

_____

_____

_____

_____

_____

_____

What is your saddest family memory growing up?

_____

_____

_____

_____

_____

_____

Is there an especially close family member you have lost? Do they often come to mind?

_____

_____

_____

_____

_____

_____

_____

What do you remember most about the birth of your children?

_____

_____

_____

_____

_____

_____

What traits or characteristics do your children exhibit that remind you of yourself, your parents, aunts or uncles, grandparents or great grandparents?

_____

_____

_____

_____

_____

_____

_____

Is there a talent your children or nieces/nephews have that may have been passed down through the generations?

_____
_____
_____
_____
_____
_____
_____

What one word best describes your life up to this point? Why?

_____
_____
_____
_____
_____
_____
_____

What words do you think best describes the lives of your children? Why?

_____
_____
_____
_____
_____
_____
_____

What do you recall about the day your grandchildren were born?

_____

_____

_____

_____

_____

_____

_____

How do you see your children doing in their roles as parents?

_____

_____

_____

_____

_____

_____

Are your children using the same child rearing techniques you used with them?

_____

_____

_____

_____

_____

_____

_____

What have your grandchildren accomplished that you are you especially proud of, and what special talents do you see in them?

_____

_____

_____

_____

_____

_____

_____

If you have great grandchildren, share your feelings about them. What are their names? When were they born?

_____

_____

_____

_____

_____

_____

_____

What family traits do you see in your grandchildren and great nieces and great nephews?

_____

_____

_____

_____

_____

_____

Have your children or grandchildren reached adulthood? If not, how do you imagine their future? If they are grown up, has the future you imagined for them come true? How is it the same or different?

_____

_____

_____

_____

_____

_____

_____

What has been your proudest moment as a parent?

_____

_____

_____

_____

_____

_____

29. Home Sweet Home

Describe the homes in which your grandparents lived in when they were children. Do you have information on your great grandparents' homes? Are there any similarities between the generations?

_____

_____

_____

_____

_____

_____

_____

Have you ever visited the country, city or hometown where your grandparents or great grandparents lived as children? How did it feel to you?

_____

_____

_____

_____

_____

_____

Have you ever been to visit your parents' childhood homes?

_____

_____

_____

_____

_____

_____

What were the circumstances around your birth? Where were you born?

_____

_____

_____

_____

_____

_____

_____

Was your first childhood home a house, an apartment, a condo, a farm etc.? Describe it as you remember it.

_____

_____

_____

_____

_____

_____

Were there any special items, features, furniture in the home?

_____

_____

_____

_____

_____

_____

_____

Did you enjoy living in your primary childhood home?

_____

_____

_____

_____

_____

_____

_____

How many homes do you remember living in? Did your family move often?

_____

_____

_____

_____

_____

_____

_____

If your family did move, where did you move and during what years of your life?

_____

_____

_____

_____

_____

_____

_____

Is there a home that was or has been in the family for a long time?

_____

_____

_____

_____

_____

_____

_____

If so, who lives in it now?

_____

_____

_____

_____

_____

_____

Was there one home that you especially loved? Or one you especially disliked?

_____

_____

_____

_____

_____

_____

_____

Talk about people who frequently visited your home when you were young? Was it a place where friends and relatives came together for holidays?

_____

_____

_____

_____

_____

_____

Share your favorite memories of gatherings at your childhood home. Who came over and how long did they stay?

_____

_____

_____

_____

_____

_____

Describe in detail your childhood bedroom. If you had windows, what were the views?

_____

_____

_____

_____

_____

_____

Did you share your bedroom, or did you have your own? What special memories do you have about it?

_____

_____

_____

_____

_____

_____

_____

Was any room of the house considered off-limits? A room your parents did not want you to play in for fear you might mess it up.

_____

_____

_____

_____

_____

_____

_____

Was there a particular room that has holds special memories? A den? The library?

_____

_____

_____

_____

_____

_____

_____

Did your home have beautiful landscaping? Do you share a green thumb with anyone else in your family?

_____

_____

_____

_____

_____

_____

_____

Did you have a yard growing up? Were there trees to climb?

_____

_____

_____

_____

_____

_____

Was there a park or community playground nearby?

_____

_____

_____

_____

_____

_____

Did you have playhouse, fort or hideaway? How was it special?

_____

_____

_____

_____

_____

_____

Share a special memory about a neighborhood experience? Did you hold block parties or other types of gatherings? How many kids were in your neighborhood?

_____

_____

_____

_____

_____

_____

Describe what your home is like today? Do you have heirlooms, furniture or artifacts from your ancestors?

_____

_____

_____

_____

_____

_____

Are there things you will be able to pass on to your siblings, children, grandchildren or friends that will carry a special significance for them and future generations?

_____

_____

_____

_____

_____

_____

_____

Where do your siblings live? Do their homes or communities reflect your childhood experiences?

_____

_____

_____

_____

_____

_____

_____

Do you currently live near any childhood friends or friends of your family? Do the neighborhood generations continue to get together?

_____

_____

_____

_____

_____

_____

_____

Did you have a TV in your family home? What were yours and your family's favorite TV programs?

_____

_____

_____

_____

_____

_____

_____

What were the programs or shows your family watched together?

_____

_____

_____

_____

_____

_____

_____

30. Family Cars

Write down the cars you can remember your family had. Were there any that you particularly liked? Why?

_____

_____

_____

_____

_____

_____

_____

31. Family Getaways and Vacations

Did your family regularly take vacations? If so, where did your family go? Did anyone go with you? On your trips what did you do for fun?

_____

_____

_____

_____

_____

_____

Did your family make a point of visiting other relatives? Or, did your relatives go on the vacations with you?

_____

_____

_____

_____

_____

_____

_____

What memories do you have of those family vacations or gatherings? Who was there, and what do you remember about them?

_____

_____

_____

_____

_____

_____

_____

Did your family have a summer home or a favorite vacation spot?

_____

_____

_____

_____

_____

_____

_____

Were camping trips on your family's list of fun things to do?If so, what did you like most about the trips, and where did you camp?

_____

_____

_____

_____

_____

_____

_____

What was your favorite family vacation? Describe where and why it was so special for you.

_____

_____

_____

_____

_____

_____

_____

What is the longest trip you have ever made? Where did you go? What did you do?

_____

_____

_____

_____

_____

_____

_____

32. Family Animals and Pets

Did you mother or father talk about their favorite dog, cat, maybe even a horse growing up? As a child do you remember if your grandparents had pets? If so, what type and what were their names?

_____

_____

_____

_____

_____

_____

_____

Did your family have many pets? If so, describe what they were.

_____

_____

_____

_____

_____

_____

_____

What was your favorite family pet? Tell why it was your favorite.

_____

_____

_____

_____

_____

_____

_____

Do you have pets now? Is there any special significance to their names?

_____

_____

_____

_____

_____

_____

_____

33. Holidays and Gatherings

Describe a memorable holiday or gathering where your family's friends joined in the celebration. Why was it special to you?

_____

_____

_____

_____

_____

_____

_____

Did the family friends introduce a new tradition or recipe to the occasion? How did their presence add to your event and make it special?

_____

_____

_____

_____

_____

_____

_____

34. Influential Ancestors and People Who Made a Difference

Do you believe you were greatly influenced by one of your ancestors? Who was it, and what was the important lesson they taught you? Why? How did they exemplify it in their own lives?

_____

_____

_____

_____

_____

_____

_____

During your early adulthood, who were the people who had the most influence on you? Consider an older brother or sister, a teacher, a coach, relative, a friend of the family?

_____

_____

_____

_____

_____

_____

_____

Describe the people who helped you find meaning in your adult life. Look at their influence in the following areas of your life -- your religion, your major in college, your profession, and your relationships?

_____

_____

_____

_____

_____

_____

_____

Who in your family is labeled the family historian or keeper of the family facts?

_____

_____

_____

_____

_____

_____

Do you have a role model or mentor? Was there someone who guided you through school or your career? Describe them.

_____

_____

_____

_____

_____

_____

How have your relationships to your closest relatives blossomed or changed over your adult years?

_____

_____

_____

_____

_____

_____

_____

Of all your family relationships which one has evolved and changed the most significantly? Is it with a parent, sibling, aunt, uncle, cousin?

_____

_____

_____

_____

_____

_____

_____

Describe what your relationship was like years ago with this person, and how does it stand today.

_____

_____

_____

_____

_____

_____

_____

35. Play and Fun Times

What do you know about your mother's and father's childhood? What did they do when they were bored? What were some of their childhood toys?

_____

_____

_____

_____

_____

_____

_____

As a child growing up, where did you go for to play and have fun? A community pool, friend's house, neighborhood park, nearby forest, etc.?

_____

_____

_____

_____

_____

_____

_____

36. Dating and Marriage

Grandparents

Do you know how your great grandparents or grandparents met each other?

_____

_____

_____

_____

_____

_____

What were their proposals like? How your grandfather(s) proposed to your grandmother(s)?

_____

_____

_____

_____

_____

_____

Parents

How did your parents meet each other? How did your father ask
your mother to marry him?

_____

_____

_____

_____

_____

_____

_____

Siblings

What were the circumstances around your brothers' and sisters'
marriages?

_____

_____

_____

_____

_____

_____

_____

You

Were there any family rules about dating when you grew up? How old were you when you started dating? Do you remember your first date or kiss?

_____

_____

_____

_____

_____

_____

_____

How did you meet your spouse, partner or significant other?

_____

_____

_____

_____

_____

_____

_____

What was it like when they proposed to you? When and where did it happen? How?

_____

_____

_____

_____

_____

_____

_____

Have you, your spouse or partner been married more than once?

_____

_____

_____

_____

_____

_____

_____

Wedding Day

When and where did you get married? What special memory stands out from your wedding day?

_____

_____

_____

_____

_____

_____

_____

Describe your wedding ceremony, event or celebration. Who were the people in your wedding party? Where did you go on your honeymoon?

_____

_____

_____

_____

_____

_____

_____

37. Rituals and Traditions

Ritual and tradition are important facets of our lives. Traditions connect us in a common endeavor. Like families who have a common goal. Traditions are the glue that bonds a family together. They provide the common ground around which a family revolves. Passed on customs originated by your ancestors are priceless. They form a lifelong connection from you to your relatives. The rituals help your family members appreciate the legacies that are passed on to future generations. It's comforting to keep traditions in a family ones they can depend on always to remain the same.

Day-to-Day Rituals

List some of the everyday events you remember growing up. Did you eat dinner together every night? What happened when it was time to go to bed? Baths, stories, music, prayers?

_____

_____

_____

_____

_____

_____

_____

What did these habits or rituals mean to you, and how are passing them along today to your family?

_____

_____

_____

_____

_____

_____

_____

Did you regularly go to church or synagogue? Did you have any daily religious practices? What about on holidays?

_____

_____

_____

_____

_____

_____

How do you remember feeling about your family's religious or spiritual commitments? Do you carry these traditions on today?

_____

_____

_____

_____

_____

_____

Do you remember if your parents sang to you or said a prayer with you before you went to sleep?

_____

_____

_____

_____

_____

_____

_____

Of the people you grew up with, who would you attribute teaching you the trait of gratitude or appreciation?

_____

_____

_____

_____

_____

_____

Based on how you grew up, do you have a special place you take your children, nieces, nephews or family friends today?

_____

_____

_____

_____

_____

_____

What happened on weekends in your family? Did you have a favorite outing? A visit to your cousins' home in the country? Sunday brunch with your grandparents at the country club? A ride in the car to the city?

_____

_____

_____

_____

_____

_____

What did you do when you were out of school for the summer? Do you remember an especially wonderful summer during your childhood? Explain.

_____

_____

_____

_____

_____

_____

Was your family involved in philanthropy or volunteering in your local community?

_____

_____

_____

_____

_____

_____

If so, how did it feel to assist people less fortunate than yourself? Did this exposure to inspire you to volunteer in your adult life?

_____

_____

_____

_____

_____

_____

_____

Did your family have certain ways or rituals to stay in touch with one another? Examples would be -- call one another each Sunday afternoon, write letters, create a family web page, hold family reunions?

_____

_____

_____

_____

_____

_____

_____

What new traditions would you like to start in your own family based on your childhood?

_____

_____

_____

_____

_____

_____

_____

Birthday Parties and Celebrations

What were the birthday rituals in your family? Did the birthday person awaken to a Happy Birthday sign and balloons and was she or he able to order their special dinner menu? How did the family celebrate, and who made the cake?

_____

_____

_____

_____

_____

_____

_____

Describe one of your favorite birthdays. Who was there? Where and what did you do for the day? What was the best ever birthday present you received? Who gave it to you?

_____

_____

_____

_____

_____

_____

_____

Holiday Traditions and Rituals

Detail your family's holiday traditions, did you make Christmas cookies? Did you create handmade ornaments? Light the menorah together? Have a backyard Easter egg hunt, or invite the neighbors over for a barbeque on July 4th?

_____

_____

_____

_____

_____

_____

_____

Of all your traditions which ones are you sure you would you like to pass on to your children and grandchildren?

_____

_____

_____

_____

_____

_____

_____

Of all the holiday gifts you ever gave, what was your favorite? What was the best gift you received, and who gave it to you?

_____

_____

_____

_____

_____

_____

_____

What traditions did your family have for the Fourth of July? Wash and wax the family car? Go to the fireworks at the fairgrounds?

_____

_____

_____

_____

_____

_____

_____

How did your family celebrate Thanksgiving? Who did the cooking?

_____

_____

_____

_____

_____

_____

_____

What was your family's absolute most favorite Christmas or Hanukkah tradition? The season would not be complete without doing this ritual.

_____

_____

_____

_____

_____

_____

_____

Times and people change -- how have your holiday rituals and traditions changed over the years? Did you start any new ones?

_____

_____

_____

_____

_____

_____

As a child growing up what were your favorite holidays? What family customs or foods did you enjoy the most?

_____

_____

_____

_____

_____

_____

Describe a few holiday memories that were so special or impor tant that your family still talks about them.

_____

_____

_____

_____

_____

_____

Try to recall any funny things that happened at holiday times.
Who was the family entertainer at your gatherings?

_____

_____

_____

_____

_____

_____

_____

What types of foods did your family prepare and eat during the
holidays? Were there ethnic specialties based on your heritage?

_____

_____

_____

_____

_____

_____

Were special holiday decorations an important part of your
family's history? Did your parents hang lights on the outside of
your home?

_____

_____

_____

_____

_____

_____

What other relatives, friends and neighbors came over for your family's celebration?

_____

_____

_____

_____

_____

_____

_____

Did the town or city you grew up in celebrate the holidays as a community? If so, how did your family take part in the events?

_____

_____

_____

_____

_____

_____

_____

What was gift giving like in your family? Did you receive gifts from your extended family? Did your parents have you write thank you notes?

_____

_____

_____

_____

_____

_____

_____

How have the holidays changed over the years? Would you like to see some of the traditional rituals come back?

_____

_____

_____

_____

_____

_____

_____

38. Food, Meals and Dining

What was your favorite meal as a child? What made it your
favorite meal? What were your favorite foods?

_____

_____

_____

_____

_____

_____

Did you all eat together as a family each evening? Who did the
cooking? What would be a typical family dinner?

_____

_____

_____

_____

_____

_____

Did you all go out to eat often? If so, what restaurant or type of
food did your family like to eat when you went out for dinner?

_____

_____

_____

_____

_____

_____

Food brings back great memories. For example was your grandmother's famous chocolate chip cookie or other family tried and
true recipes passed down to you?

_____

_____

_____

_____

_____

_____

_____

39. Family Heirlooms Gems, Jewelry, Furniture and Antiques

Did your family have a particularly prized heirloom? Explain what, where it came from, why was it important, and how did your family come by it.

_____
_____
_____
_____
_____
_____
_____

What are some of the other heirlooms passed down? If an heirloom was a piece of jewelry, tell who originally wore the jewelry? Why was it given? Who received the piece and why?

_____
_____
_____
_____
_____
_____
_____

Were there ever any family disputes over heirlooms -- who got the items and why? If so, are you making sure there won't be disputes over heirlooms you leave to family members?

_____
_____
_____
_____
_____
_____
_____

Were there any pieces of furniture, work tools or kitchen utensils passed down? Mention what they were and give information on who first brought them into the family. How were they used over the generations?

_____
_____
_____
_____
_____
_____
_____

How did your family hold on to these family treasures? Was a particular family member designated as the historian or manager of items? Was your family ever at risk of losing any of these treasures? If so, how did they hang on to it?

_____
_____
_____
_____
_____
_____
_____

Do you recall if there was a family heirloom that was lost or badly damaged? What was it, and how did your family react to this loss?

_____

_____

_____

_____

_____

_____

_____

40. Your Family Vision

You have spent most of this book exploring your family history and looking back over your life -- your childhood memories, exciting moments, challenges and major turning points. You've explored family rituals and traditions, celebrations and events that evoke memories tightly held in your heart. Now is the time to answer some of the fundamental questions that will shape your dreams and those you have for your children, their children and the generations to come. Here are some questions to help you examine what lies ahead as you continue to preserve traditions, yet think about the hopes and dreams you have in your heart for the generations to come.

What wisdom or counsel about life that you learned from your ancestors would you like future generations to remember?

_____

_____

_____

_____

_____

_____

_____

What hard earned lesson do you want to make sure your children and grandchildren understand?

_____

_____

_____

_____

_____

_____

What aspirations do you have for your brothers and sisters? What can you do to help make sure these hopes come to pass?

_____

_____

_____

_____

_____

_____

_____

What are your highest hopes for your children? What can you do to make sure they are realized?

_____

_____

_____

_____

_____

_____

_____

Do you have dreams for your nieces and nephews? If so, have you thought about how you could help them achieve their dreams?

_____

_____

_____

_____

_____

_____

_____

If you have grandchildren, what are your grand hopes for them? What can you do to help and assist them realize these hopes?

_____

_____

_____

_____

_____

_____

_____

Are there dreams of your own that you would like to realize? What conscious efforts are you doing to make them happen?

_____

_____

_____

_____

_____

_____

If you have a spouse, partner or significant other, what dreams of theirs do you want to come true for them? What can you do to help them make their aspirations a reality?

_____

_____

_____

_____

_____

_____

Of all the things about life you learned from your parents, what is
the most important thing you hope to pass on to your children?

_____

_____

_____

_____

_____

_____

_____

What is your vision over the next 10 years? What would like to
see happen for your family?

_____

_____

_____

_____

_____

_____

_____

What is your vision over the next 20 years? What would like to
see happen for your family?

_____

_____

_____

_____

_____

_____

_____

41.Tracing, Tracking and Recording Your Ancestors

If you don't know where to start to trace your ancestors, look at your own face in the mirror. Your immediate family is a key to your genealogical past. The best way to begin your family search is to start with yourself and work backward. The first step is to start with a basic generation chart. This becomes your road map to creating your ancestors' genealogical path. Place yourself at the beginning and branch back one set of parents at a time. Examples of generational charts are easily available on the Internet. Other key information about each family member, in addition to full names, are their birth date, place of birth, date and place of marriage, date and place of death. This compiled information helps immensely in researching ancestors. In the United States, states and counties organize most family information. There are also many websites and CD-ROM programs available to help you. Now that public records are accessible online, tracing your family tree is just a click away.

Sources to Help You Compile Family Record Information

Use the below sources and strategies for ideas and ways to help in your research. Make sure to write down notes or facts that might help you along the way. For example, your father called his grandmother Mamiere. This might play a role in identifying information on your great great grandmother.

Church Records

Synagogues and parish churches often document records of birth, marriages and deaths. The religious administrative offices may have records you could use, such as data information from the archives of the Diocese or Archdiocese of local Catholic Churches. Check where family members were married. Do you know what church, synagogue or house of worship they were affiliated with? Over what years they might they have attended?

Information about the, who, what, where and when of baptisms / communions / bar or bat mitzvahs/marriages can be very helpful for your research.

Private Collections and Newspapers

Do you know if there are any private collections or published family histories? Sometimes families donate their papers to private museum collections. Serious genealogists make it a point to examine and research these resources.

Newspapers are also an excellent resource. Obituaries, birth and marriage announcements often provide accurate genealogical source information. Based on your family history's timeline, write down some of the newspaper headlines you might find during key years. Who was President? What laws or amendments were being passed?

Census Records

Census and county records are another excellent source of information. The U.S. Census Bureau takes a national census every ten years. Create a time line showing when and where your ancestors were born to help trace your family's generations.

City County Clerk Records

An ideal place to find detailed information is at the family member's city of residence county clerks offices. Land and property deeds, voter registration, polls, oaths, bonds, marriage licenses, divorce decrees, business licenses, brand, mining records, notary records and assessor's office tax records are all excellent sources of information. Make detailed notes of any of these records in your possession before you begin your search.

Military, Legal Documents and Diary Sources

Military records give a lot of information regarding family members. Wills, last testaments, journals and diaries, are valuable sources of personal information. If you have access to any of these documents, what do they tell you about your family?

Miscellaneous Sources

Probate Offices: for case files, wills, testaments, guardianships and adoptions

District Court Record or Civil and Criminal Docket Books: for legal cases

Naturalization Records: Declaration and Intention; Petition for Naturalization; Certificate of Naturalization;

Land Grants and Conveyances

These records chart the distribution of land, including records of the Surveyor General and the Court of Private Land Claims. These records are important in that they list land grantees, heirs, complete family names and relationships. Make notes here if you have access to any of these documents.

Internet Genealogy Sources

To trace living extended family relatives, the best place to search is in cities' White Pages or on the Internet. Since many of the above listed records are online, the Internet is an amazing source to research your ancestors. Some online sources include:

> www.censusfetch.com
> www.ancestry.com
> www.genealogy.com
> www.rootsweb.com
> www.ellisisland.org
> www.familysearch.org
> www.worldfamilies.net

Use the space below to list other online resources and URL addresses.

_____

_____

_____

_____

_____

_____

_____

42. Family Photographs

Family photos tell stories that may not be recorded or captured anywhere else. In a photo of a family picnic, an exact moment in time is captured. Were sisters holding hands? Was your aunt scowling at your mother cutting the dessert pie? Photos document expressions that reflect moods and feelings. Is there a particular family photo that stands out in your mind? If so, why does it hold so much meaning for you?

Photo Handling and Storage Tips

When storing and handling family photos, please remember they can be damaged by time, too much light and extremes in temperature and humidity. Store your photos carefully in an area where the temperature is steady. Try to avoid extremes found in attics (heat) and basements (humidity).Now that we are in the digital age, we no longer need the negatives to have copies made. Make sure to make multiple copies of your favorite family photos and send them to relatives living in other parts of the country. Document the information in photos so that your family members understand the who, what, where, why and when of the people in the photograph.

Make note of some other family photos you have in your possession and the people you might like to share with them. For example, you might have a photo of a grandparent that possibly one or more of your cousins might also enjoy.

_____

_____

_____

_____

_____

Back to the Future

We hope you have enjoyed this opportunity to revisit your family's history, a treasure chest of loved ones' experiences and wisdom. You have retraced many steps. You have taken many looks backward into your past and no doubt encountered some side glances as well. When you asked for help, we are sure your relatives shared their memories and recollections of good times and sad times. The culmination of this journey is this precious collection of family stories, wit and wisdom, rituals and traditions. You have created a lens of love for all of your family members to look both at your ancestry and your future visions. By sharing your heritage, you have given the next generation a glimpse of what's yet to come. You've created a bridge for your children and future generations to take your family values, fun family quirks, pastimes and rituals, and carry the meaning of those stories into the future. Family will always be forever. With this book you will always be reminded about how those you love created the bloodline ties that bind.

Quote

The great gift of family life is to be intimately acquainted with people you might never even introduce yourself to, had life not done it for you.

~Kendall Hailey

Appendix

Your Family Portrait

Your Full Given Name

_____

Place & Date of Birth

_____

Mother's Full Name

_____

Place & Date of Birth

_____

Father's Full Name

_____

Place & Date of Birth

_____

Name of Paternal Great-Great Grandmother

_____

Place & Date of Birth

_____

Name of Paternal Great-Great Grandfather

_____

Place & Date of Birth

_____

Name of Maternal Great-Great Grandmother

_____

Place & Date of Birth

_____

Name of Maternal Great-Great Grandfather

Place & Date of Birth

Name of Paternal Great-Grandmother

Place & Date of Birth

Name of Paternal Great-Grandfather

Place & Date of Birth

Name of Maternal Great-Grandmother

Place & Date of Birth

Name of Maternal Great-Grandfather

Place & Date of Birth

Name of Paternal Grandmother

Place & Date of Birth

Name of Paternal Grandfather

Place & Date of Birth

Name of Maternal Grandmother

_____

Place & Date of Birth

_____

Name of Maternal Grandfather

_____

Place & Date of Birth

_____

Name of Spouse

_____

Place & Date of Birth

_____

Name of Spouse's Paternal Great-Great Grandmother

_____

Place & Date of Birth

_____

Name of Spouse's Paternal Great-Great Grandfather

_____

Place & Date of Birth

_____

Name of Spouse's Maternal Great-Great Grandmother

_____

Place & Date of Birth

_____

Name of Spouse's Maternal Great-Great Grandfather

_____

Place & Date of Birth

_____

Name of Spouse's Paternal Great-Grandmother

Place & Date of Birth

Name of Spouse's Paternal Great-Grandfather

Place & Date of Birth

Name of Spouse's Maternal Great-Grandmother

Place & Date of Birth

Name of Spouse's Maternal Great-Grandfather

Place & Date of Birth

Name of Spouse's Paternal Grandmother

Place & Date of Birth

Name of Spouse's Paternal Grandfather

Place & Date of Birth

Name of Spouse's Maternal Grandmother

Place & Date of Birth

Name of Spouse's Maternal Grandfather

_____

Place & Date of Birth

_____

Names of Your Children

_____

_____

Place(s) & Date(s) of Birth

_____

_____

_____

Names of Your Grandchildren

_____

_____

Place(s) & Date(s) of Birth

_____

_____

_____

Names of Your Great-Grandchildren

_____

_____

Place(s) & Date(s) of Birth

_____

_____

_____

Names of Your Siblings & Their Spouses

_____

_____

Place(s) & Date(s) of Birth

_____

_____

Names of Your Spouse's Siblings & Their Spouses

_____

_____

Place(s) & Date(s) of Birth

_____

_____

Names of Your Nieces & Nephews

_____

_____

Place(s) & Date(s) of Birth

_____

_____

Names of Your Great-Nieces & Great-Nephews

_____

Place(s) & Date(s) of Birth

_____

_____

www.ingramcontent.com/pod-product-compliance
Lightning Source LLC
Chambersburg PA
CBHW030638150426
42813CB00050B/98